Ready-to-Use

CARTOONS
for Church
Publications

Ready-to-Use CARTOONS for Church Publications

Phil Jackson

BAKER BOOK HOUSE
Grand Rapids, Michigan 49516

An Instant Supply
of Ready-to-Use Cartoons

There's nothing like a dash of humor to put some sparkle in a newsletter or home bulletin. Soon your members will check the cartoon before they read the rest of the material.

The cartoons appear in two sizes so that they may be quickly inserted without enlargement or reduction in that open spot in a newsletter. The cartoons may be used by local churches without writing for permission.

Phil Jackson has a knack of seeing humor in everyday situations. With a gentle touch he puts his finger on human foibles and frailties. Often there is a subtle but unmistakable "sermon" in the cartoon. Phil intended that and he'll be glad you spotted it.

"WE BROUGHT A HAM, SCALLOPED POTATOES, A SALAD....HE CAN PREACH AS LONG AS HE WANTS TO TODAY."

"OH, MRS. WAGNER, 'YE OF LITTLE FAITH.'"

"SHHHHH... HE'S PRACTICING FOR RETIREMENT."

"NOW, REMEMBER, SECOND ROW, THIRD ONE IN, THAT'S YOUR PRUNE JUICE."

"OH, MRS. WAGNER, 'YE OF LITTLE FAITH.'"

"WE BROUGHT A HAM, SCALLOPED POTATOES, A SALAD... HE CAN PREACH AS LONG AS HE WANTS TO TODAY."

"NOW, REMEMBER, SECOND ROW, THIRD ONE IN, THAT'S YOUR PRUNE JUICE."

"SHHHHH... HE'S PRACTICING FOR RETIREMENT."

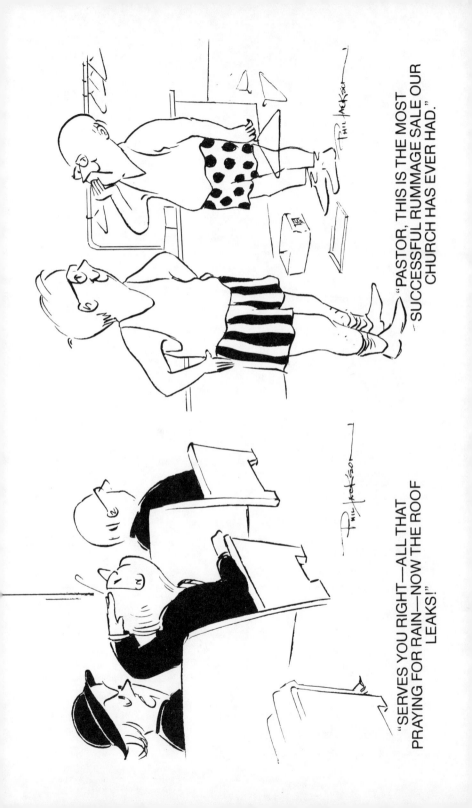

"PASTOR, THIS IS THE MOST SUCCESSFUL RUMMAGE SALE OUR CHURCH HAS EVER HAD."

"SERVES YOU RIGHT—ALL THAT PRAYING FOR RAIN—NOW THE ROOF LEAKS!"

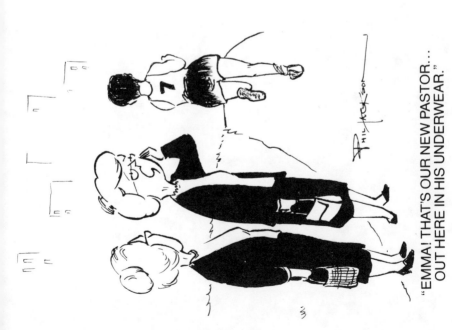

"EMMA! THAT'S OUR NEW PASTOR....
OUT HERE IN HIS UNDERWEAR."

"SERVES YOU RIGHT—ALL THAT PRAYING FOR RAIN—NOW THE ROOF LEAKS!"

"PASTOR, THIS IS THE MOST SUCCESSFUL RUMMAGE SALE OUR CHURCH HAS EVER HAD."

"EMMA! THAT'S OUR NEW PASTOR... OUT HERE IN HIS UNDERWEAR."

"CHANGE, MA'AM?"

"THANK YOU, LORD, FOR MEDICAL SCIENCE—PILLS TO HELP MY SENILITY... HELP ME, LORD, WHEN DID HE SAY TO TAKE 'EM?"

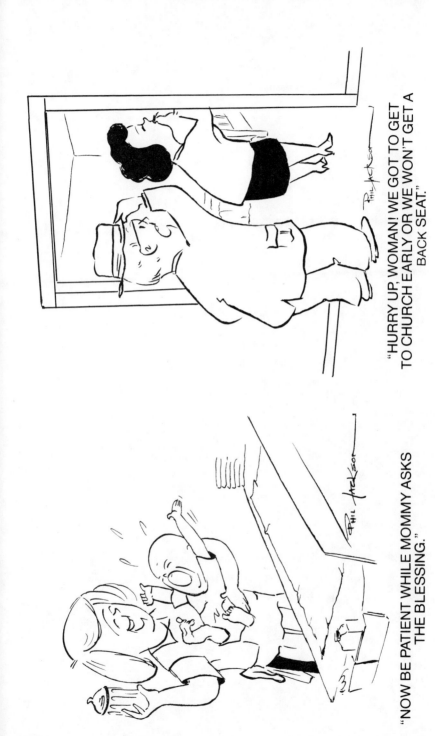

"HURRY UP, WOMAN! WE GOT TO GET TO CHURCH EARLY OR WE WON'T GET A BACK SEAT."

"NOW BE PATIENT WHILE MOMMY ASKS THE BLESSING."

"NOW BE PATIENT WHILE MOMMY ASKS
THE BLESSING."

"HURRY UP, WOMAN! WE GOT TO GET
TO CHURCH EARLY OR WE WON'T GET A
BACK SEAT."

"THANK YOU, LORD, FOR MEDICAL
SCIENCE—PILLS TO HELP MY
SENILITY... HELP ME, LORD, WHEN DID
HE SAY TO TAKE 'EM?"

"CHANGE, MA'AM?"

"WHAT'S YOUR GAME PLAN FOR THIS MORNING SERVICE, PASTOR?"

"OH, WILBUR, I'VE BEEN PRAYING YOU WOULD FIX THIS LAMP."

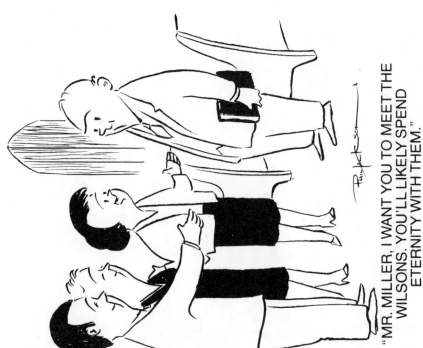

"MR. MILLER, I WANT YOU TO MEET THE WILSONS. YOU'LL LIKELY SPEND ETERNITY WITH THEM."

"OH, WILBUR, I'VE BEEN PRAYING YOU
WOULD FIX THIS LAMP."

"WHAT'S YOUR GAME PLAN FOR THIS
MORNING SERVICE, PASTOR?"

"MR. MILLER, I WANT YOU TO MEET THE
WILSONS. YOU'LL LIKELY SPEND
ETERNITY WITH THEM."

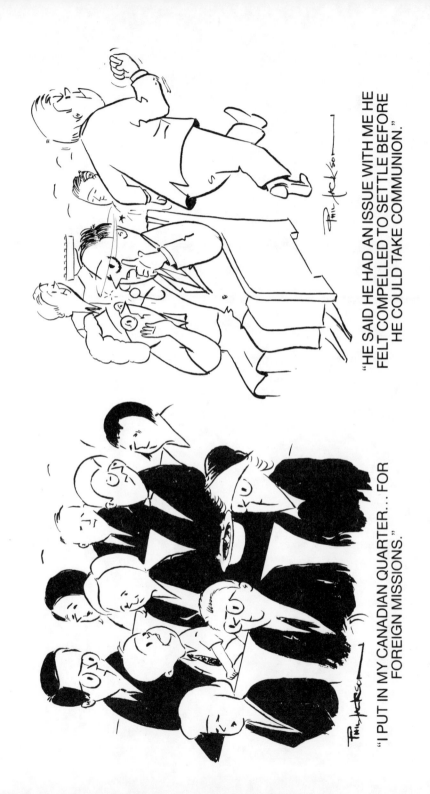

"HE SAID HE HAD AN ISSUE WITH ME HE FELT COMPELLED TO SETTLE BEFORE HE COULD TAKE COMMUNION."

"I PUT IN MY CANADIAN QUARTER... FOR FOREIGN MISSIONS."

"I DO WISH YOU WOULD PRAY FOR WILBUR'S EYESIGHT... THESE HEADLIGHTS DRIVE HIM CRAZY."

"NO, THANKS! I'M DRIVING."

"I PUT IN MY CANADIAN QUARTER… FOR
FOREIGN MISSIONS."

"HE SAID HE HAD AN ISSUE WITH ME HE
FELT COMPELLED TO SETTLE BEFORE
HE COULD TAKE COMMUNION."

"NO, THANKS! I'M DRIVING."

"I DO WISH YOU WOULD PRAY FOR
WILBUR'S EYESIGHT… THESE
HEADLIGHTS DRIVE HIM CRAZY."

HH
June 1991

"PLEASE BE PATIENT... OUR SPEAKER HAS A SCREW LOOSE."

"LORD... DON'T YOU HAVE A LITTLE CHURCH IN FLORIDA, ARIZONA, GEORGIA, OR MAYBE IN THE CAROLINAS WHERE YOU NEED THIS LITTLE FAT COUNTRY PREACHER?"

"BETTER RUN! HERE COMES SISTER BESSIE AND SHE'S ON THAT ROMANS 16:16 KICK AGAIN!"

"BUT, MISS KELLY, IS IT AGAINST THE LAW, EVEN WHEN I AM PRAYING FOR YOU?"

"LORD... DON'T YOU HAVE A LITTLE
CHURCH IN FLORIDA, ARIZONA,
GEORGIA, OR MAYBE IN THE CAROLINAS
WHERE YOU NEED THIS LITTLE FAT
COUNTRY PREACHER?"

"PLEASE BE PATIENT... OUR SPEAKER
HAS A SCREW LOOSE."

"BUT, MISS KELLY, IS IT AGAINST THE
LAW, EVEN WHEN I AM PRAYING FOR
YOU?"

"BETTER RUN! HERE COMES SISTER
BESSIE AND SHE'S ON THAT ROMANS
16:16 KICK AGAIN!"

"MA'AM, I AM A CHRISTIAN TOO. WHERE IS THAT VERSE THAT SAYS, 'THE LORD LOVES A CHEERFUL FORGIVER'?"

"STRIKE? YOU'RE BLIND! YOU JERK! YOU BUM! YOU DON'T KNOW WHAT YOU'RE DOING, PASTOR!"

"COULD YOU GIVE US SEATS IN THE BACK? WE'RE LEAVING FOR THE BEACH RIGHT AFTER THE SERVICE."

"THEY REALLY KNOW HOW TO MAKE A FELLER FEEL WELCOME IN THIS CHURCH."

"STRIKE? YOU'RE BLIND! YOU JERK! YOU BUM! YOU DON'T KNOW WHAT YOU'RE DOING, PASTOR!"

"MA'AM, I AM A CHRISTIAN TOO. WHERE IS THAT VERSE THAT SAYS, 'THE LORD LOVES A CHEERFUL FORGIVER'?"

"THEY REALLY KNOW HOW TO MAKE A FELLER FEEL WELCOME IN THIS CHURCH."

"COULD YOU GIVE US SEATS IN THE BACK? WE'RE LEAVING FOR THE BEACH RIGHT AFTER THE SERVICE."

HH 1991
June

HH 1991
~~June~~ May

"EDNA, THE PASTOR HAS COME FOR A VISIT!"

"IT'S A REAL MIRACLE THAT WILBUR CAN DRIVE AT ALL. YOU KNOW, HE CAN HARDLY SEE TO THE EDGE OF THE ROAD."

"OF COURSE, IT WAS A GOOD SERMON ON GOING TO HEAVEN, BUT HE WANTED TO GET UP A BUS LOAD TO LEAVE TONIGHT!"

"WATCH WHAT HE PUTS IN THE OFFERING PLATE. HE USUALLY GIVES GREAT GIFTS."

"IT'S A REAL MIRACLE THAT WILBUR CAN DRIVE AT ALL. YOU KNOW, HE CAN HARDLY SEE TO THE EDGE OF THE ROAD."

"EDNA, THE PASTOR HAS COME FOR A VISIT!"

"WATCH WHAT HE PUTS IN THE OFFERING PLATE. HE USUALLY GIVES GREAT GIFTS."

"OF COURSE, IT WAS A GOOD SERMON ON GOING TO HEAVEN, BUT HE WANTED TO GET UP A BUS LOAD TO LEAVE TONIGHT!"

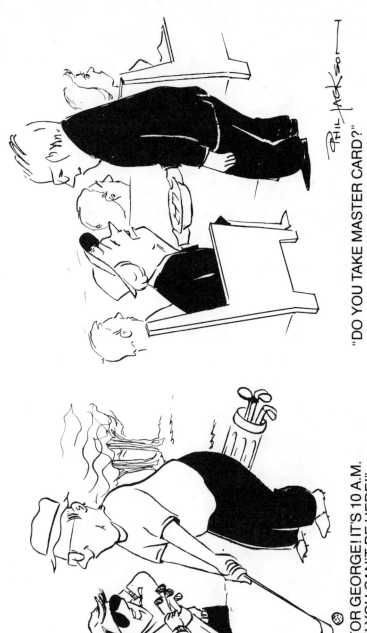

"DO YOU TAKE MASTER CARD?"

"OH, PASTOR GEORGE! IT'S 10 A.M. SUNDAY! YOU CAN'T BE HERE!"

"SAY! I DO LIKE THIS DAVID AND GOLIATH EPISODE. HE HAD HIS WHOLE DEFENSE BUDGET IN A HANDFUL OF ROCKS."

"HE JOGGED ALL THE WAY TO CHURCH THIS MORNING."

"OH, PASTOR GEORGE! IT'S 10 A.M. SUNDAY! YOU CAN'T BE HERE!"

"DO YOU TAKE MASTER CARD?"

"SAY! I DO LIKE THIS DAVID AND GOLIATH EPISODE. HE HAD HIS WHOLE DEFENSE BUDGET IN A HANDFUL OF ROCKS."

"HE JOGGED ALL THE WAY TO CHURCH THIS MORNING."

"THE BEST PART OF THE WHOLE SERVICE WAS WHERE EVERYONE SAID, 'A-MAN!! A-MAN!! A-MAN!!'"

"ALL RIGHT! ARE ALL THE CANDIDATES FOR BAPTISM PRESENT?"

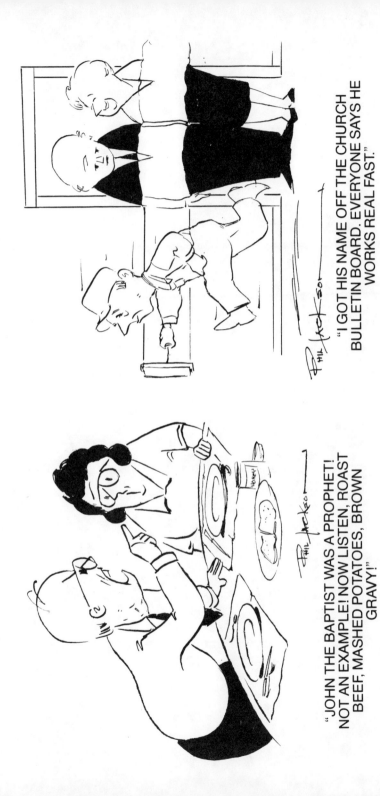

"ALL RIGHT! ARE ALL THE CANDIDATES
FOR BAPTISM PRESENT?"

"THE BEST PART OF THE WHOLE
SERVICE WAS WHERE EVERYONE SAID,
'A-MAN!! A-MAN!!'"

"JOHN THE BAPTIST WAS A PROPHET!
NOT AN EXAMPLE! NOW LISTEN, ROAST
BEEF, MASHED POTATOES, BROWN
GRAVY!"

"I GOT HIS NAME OFF THE CHURCH
BULLETIN BOARD. EVERYONE SAYS HE
WORKS REAL FAST."

"GUESS THE JACKSONS OVERSLEPT AGAIN!"

"HOME RUN!!!"

"ISN'T THIS THE TIME WE COME TO PRAY FOR RAIN?"

"GUESS THE JACKSONS OVERSLEPT
AGAIN!"

"ISN'T THIS THE TIME WE COME TO
PRAY FOR RAIN?"

"HOME RUN!!!"

"GRANDMA, WHEN GRANDPA WAS A LITTLE KID LIKE US, DID HE EVER GO TO SUNDAY SCHOOL AND SUCK HIS THUMB?"

"HE WENT TO SLEEP DURING THE FIRST HYMN OF THE MORNING. I'M GOING TO LEAVE HIM THERE UNTIL AFTER THE SERVICE THIS EVENING."

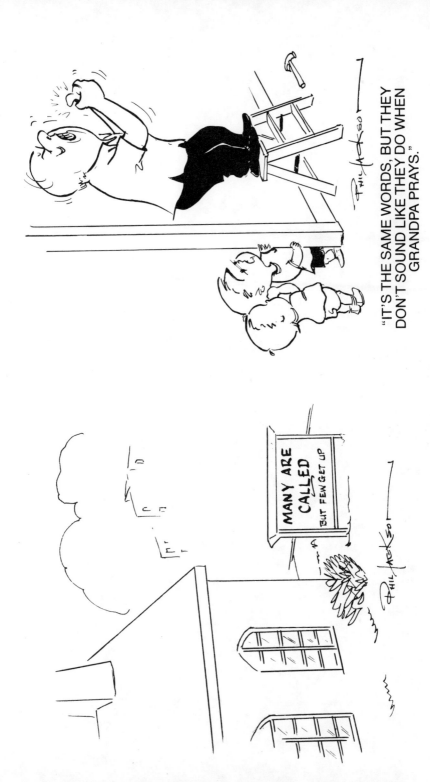

"IT'S THE SAME WORDS, BUT THEY DON'T SOUND LIKE THEY DO WHEN GRANDPA PRAYS."

MANY ARE CALLED
BUT FEW GET UP

"HE WENT TO SLEEP DURING THE FIRST HYMN OF THE MORNING. I'M GOING TO LEAVE HIM THERE UNTIL AFTER THE SERVICE THIS EVENING."

"GRANDMA, WHEN GRANDPA WAS A LITTLE KID LIKE US, DID HE EVER GO TO SUNDAY SCHOOL AND SUCK HIS THUMB?"

MANY ARE CALLED
BUT FEW GET UP

"IT'S THE SAME WORDS, BUT THEY DON'T SOUND LIKE THEY DO WHEN GRANDPA PRAYS."

"I AM THE HORSE'S BEHIND IN MY SUNDAY SCHOOL CLASS PLAY. AND I DON'T HAVE TO LEARN ANY WORDS."

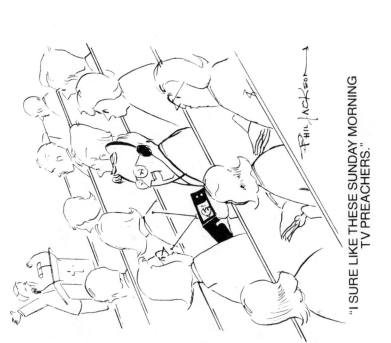

"I SURE LIKE THESE SUNDAY MORNING TV PREACHERS."

"I SURE LIKE THESE SUNDAY MORNING
TV PREACHERS."

"I AM THE HORSE'S BEHIND IN MY
SUNDAY SCHOOL CLASS PLAY. AND I
DON'T HAVE TO LEARN ANY WORDS."

"AND, GOD, DON'T LET ANYONE GET
HURT. AND HELP US TO KNOCK THEIR
HEADS OFF!"

"WHEN SHE GETS TO THAT HIGH NOTE...
LET THE MOUSE GO."

"OH, NO! HE'LL NEVER TAKE IT OFF. HE
FORGOT HIS TOUPEE THIS MORNING."

"WE'RE GOING TO START COMING TO
THE SECOND SERVICE. IT'S GETTING
HARDER AND HARDER TO GET WALTER
GOING THIS EARLY EVERY SUNDAY."

"WATSON! I KNOW HE'S PREACHING ON LOVE... BUT HELEN IS MY WIFE!"

"WOW!! I SWALLOWED A BUG ON THAT LAST HIGH NOTE."

"OH, NO! HE'LL NEVER TAKE IT OFF. HE FORGOT HIS TOUPEE THIS MORNING."

"WE'RE GOING TO START COMING TO THE SECOND SERVICE. IT'S GETTING HARDER AND HARDER TO GET WALTER GOING THIS EARLY EVERY SUNDAY."

"WOW!! I SWALLOWED A BUG ON THAT LAST HIGH NOTE."

"WATSON! I KNOW HE'S PREACHING ON LOVE... BUT HELEN IS MY WIFE!"

"JESUS' MAMA WAS REALLY GREAT! SHE LET HIM HAVE CAMELS, COWS, SHEEP, AND ALL KINDS OF ANIMALS IN HIS BEDROOM."

"YOU ALWAYS WANT ME TO BE LIKE JESUS. HE WAS BORN IN A BARN AND I BET HIS MOTHER DIDN'T MAKE HIM TAKE A BATH EVERY DAY."

"WHY DO WE PRAY, 'GOD, KEEP THIS OLD CAR GOING'? LET'S JUST PRAY FOR A NEW CAR."

"REMEMBER A COUPLE OF MONTHS AGO? YOU PRAYED GOD WOULD BLOW ALL THOSE LEAVES AWAY? WELL, YOUR PRAYER WAS JUST ANSWERED!"

"YOU ALWAYS WANT ME TO BE LIKE JESUS. HE WAS BORN IN A BARN AND I BET HIS MOTHER DIDN'T MAKE HIM TAKE A BATH EVERY DAY."

"JESUS' MAMA WAS REALLY GREAT! SHE LET HIM HAVE CAMELS, COWS, SHEEP, AND ALL KINDS OF ANIMALS IN HIS BEDROOM."

"REMEMBER A COUPLE OF MONTHS AGO? YOU PRAYED GOD WOULD BLOW ALL THOSE LEAVES AWAY? WELL, YOUR PRAYER WAS JUST ANSWERED!"

"WHY DO WE PRAY, 'GOD, KEEP THIS OLD CAR GOING'? LET'S JUST PRAY FOR A NEW CAR."

"YOU ARE RIGHT! OUT HERE NEXT TO GOD WHERE YOU CAN THINK!! WOULD YOU LIKE TO KNOW WHAT I AM THINKING?"

"THEY'RE THE DEACONS. THEY'VE COME TO PRAY AND LAY HANDS ON GRANDPA... THEY DID THAT WITH MRS. WELCH AND SHE HAD TWINS."

"PASTOR, BELIEVE ME. THAT WAS ONE
OF YOUR MOST RELAXING SERMONS."

"MAMA, GOD DIDN'T ANSWER YOUR
PRAYER. AUNT MIN IS HERE!"

"THEY'RE THE DEACONS. THEY'VE COME TO PRAY AND LAY HANDS ON GRANDPA... THEY DID THAT WITH MRS. WELCH AND SHE HAD TWINS."

"YOU ARE RIGHT! OUT HERE NEXT TO GOD WHERE YOU CAN THINK!! WOULD YOU LIKE TO KNOW WHAT I AM THINKING?"

"PASTOR, BELIEVE ME. THAT WAS ONE OF YOUR MOST RELAXING SERMONS."

"MAMA, GOD DIDN'T ANSWER YOUR PRAYER. AUNT MIN IS HERE!"

"WILLIAMS, I'VE BEEN WATCHING YOU...
YOU'RE A SNEAKIN' DEACON!!!"

"EVERT, I JUST KNOW THE LORD IS
REALLY BLESSING YOU AS YOU DRIVE
THE SUNDAY SCHOOL BUS."

"DIDN'T MARY'S AND JOSEPH'S STABLE HAVE TELEVISION OR NOTHING, GRANDPA?"

"SOCIAL SECURITY. THAT'S GRANDMA AND GRANDPA TALK AND THAT'S SOMETHING THEY DON'T DARE LET GOD TAKE CARE OF."

"EVERT, I JUST KNOW THE LORD IS REALLY BLESSING YOU AS YOU DRIVE THE SUNDAY SCHOOL BUS."

"WILLIAMS, I'VE BEEN WATCHING YOU... YOU'RE A SNEAKIN' DEACON!!!"

"DIDN'T MARY'S AND JOSEPH'S STABLE HAVE TELEVISION OR NOTHING, GRANDPA?"

"SOCIAL SECURITY. THAT'S GRANDMA AND GRANDPA TALK AND THAT'S SOMETHING THEY DON'T DARE LET GOD TAKE CARE OF."

"I DON'T KNOW WHY! I SAW THEM DO IT ON THE TV CHURCHES... AND I LIKE IT... IT'S FUN... IT FEELS GREAT!!!"

"WE ALWAYS PRAYED, 'GOD GIVE HIM KNOWLEDGE.' NOW JUST LOOK AT HIM—HE DOESN'T KNOW THE DIFFERENCE BETWEEN GRADUATION AND RETIREMENT."

"WILBUR!!! I DON'T CARE HOW MUCH ITS SNOWIN' AND BLOWIN'. YOU'VE GOTTA GO TO CHURCH!!! YOU'RE THE PREACHER!"

"I KNOW THE LORD GIVETH... BUT WHEN DOES HE TAKETH AWAAAYYY?"

"WE ALWAYS PRAYED, 'GOD GIVE HIM KNOWLEDGE.' NOW JUST LOOK AT HIM—HE DOESN'T KNOW THE DIFFERENCE BETWEEN GRADUATION AND RETIREMENT."

"I DON'T KNOW WHY! I SAW THEM DO IT ON THE TV CHURCHES... AND I LIKE IT... IT'S FUN... IT FEELS GREAT!!!"

"I KNOW THE LORD GIVETH... BUT WHEN DOES HE TAKETH AWAAAYYY?"

"WILBUR!!! I DON'T CARE HOW MUCH ITS SNOWIN' AND BLOWIN'. YOU'VE GOTTA GO TO CHURCH!!! YOU'RE THE PREACHER!"

"I THOUGHT I TOLD YOU NOT TO BRING THAT BAG OF MARBLES TO CHURCH."

"ONE FOR FIRST BAPTIST CHURCH, ONE FOR ME, TWO FOR FIRST BAPTIST CHURCH, TWO FOR ME..."

"IS JIMMY SLEEPING OVER THERE ON THE OTHER SIDE OF YOU?"

"CAN'T YOU CHEW GUM IN CHURCH LIKE THE REST OF US?"

"ONE FOR FIRST BAPTIST CHURCH, ONE
FOR ME, TWO FOR FIRST BAPTIST
CHURCH, TWO FOR ME…"

"I THOUGHT I TOLD YOU NOT TO BRING
THAT BAG OF MARBLES TO CHURCH."

"CAN'T YOU CHEW GUM IN CHURCH
LIKE THE REST OF US?"

"IS JIMMY SLEEPING OVER THERE ON
THE OTHER SIDE OF YOU?"

"THEY'RE CHRISTIANS! THEY GO TO CHURCH ALL THE TIME. THEY'RE NOT SUPPOSED TO BE HAPPY."

"BETTER CHECK OLD MR. WILSON IN THE THIRD ROW. I CAN'T TELL IF HE'S FILLED WITH THE SPIRIT OR IF HE NEEDS HELP TO FIND THE RESTROOM."

"ALL RIGHT!!! ALL RIGHT!!! I KNOW THE GAME STARTS IN 20 MINUTES."

"MY, I DO WISH HE WOULD SPEAK UP!"

"BETTER CHECK OLD MR. WILSON IN THE THIRD ROW. I CAN'T TELL IF HE'S FILLED WITH THE SPIRIT OR IF HE NEEDS HELP TO FIND THE RESTROOM."

"THEY'RE CHRISTIANS! THEY GO TO CHURCH ALL THE TIME. THEY'RE NOT SUPPOSED TO BE HAPPY."

"MY, I DO WISH HE WOULD SPEAK UP!"

"ALL RIGHT!!! ALL RIGHT!!! I KNOW THE GAME STARTS IN 20 MINUTES."